Daughter

Daughter

Poems
Cortney Davis

GRAYSON BOOKS
West Hartford, Connecticut
graysonbooks.com

Daughter
Copyright © 2021 by Cortney Davis
Published by Grayson Books
West Hartford, Connecticut
ISBN: 978-1-7364168-3-9
Library of Congress Control Number: 2021913402

Interior & Cover Design by Cindy Stewart
Cover Photo by Serafima Lazarenko on Unsplash
Author Photo by Marie Svalstedt

for my daughter
December 1966 - April 2021

and for her four children
her beautiful legacy

these poems of grief, of joy, of deep abiding love

Acknowledgments

My gratitude to the editors of the following journals in which these poems first appeared, sometimes in earlier versions:

Ars Medica: "Croup Weather"

Bellevue Literary Review: "Everything in Life Is Divided"

Crazyhorse: "How I Imagine It"

Hartford Courant: "To a Daughter, Moved Away"

Heliotrope: "Parturition"

Hobo Jungle: "Little Children then, on My Lap"

Intima: a Journal of Narrative Medicine: "It Was the Second Patient of the Day"

inScribe: "Walking along the Water's Edge"

Letter among Friends: "Taking the Children Back"

Sojourner: "On Not Loving Your Children"

St. Katherine Review: "Winter Solstice"

Contents

I.

My heart was split, and a flower
appeared, and grace sprang up…

—The Odes of Solomon

Walking along the Water's Edge

I was walking along the water's edge with you,
soon-to-be born daughter, inside me. You knew
nothing yet of the world but what I told you, and so

I talked to you all day—mornings with the first heat,
afternoons when the breeze stopped
and Canyon Lake reflected an immense blue sky.

We walked through brush and dust searching
for colors: the yellow spikes of Bulbine; scrub oaks
casting shadows dark as blood. *All this beauty*, I'd say,

yet we know less than the owl or the coyote at dusk.
And we'd walk on, naming everything as small
as the spiders hiding under stones, or endless

as the land that jutted into the water like God's hand.
Once a scorpion crossed our path; once
a bobcat looked down at us but didn't pounce.

Another time we lay down under sun so hot
we fell asleep, and later waded a moss-green
stream that leapt with water bugs. I told you

about the sea—how once I swam in it,
while you swam in me. Do you remember
how we floated in the lake until I saw

the water snakes gliding toward us, glossy
and quick, long bodies held upright? Then,
we escaped. Then, I could keep you safe.

Parturition

Coyotes quarrel with the Long Night Moon.
I'm young. My first child is due.

I can't sleep. Scorpions hurry
to hide in every crack. I worry—

will I be wiser than my parents?
Back home, my mother wakes—

her daughter's face
among dogs and rattlesnakes.

She writes me: *Scorpions invade my dreams.*
Are you in danger?

But I love the coyotes' dirge,
their hollow outline on the ridge,

and how the wild boar stink, wet with rain.
At 3 a.m., my labor pains begin.

Newborn: Winter Morning in Texas

That December morning there was frost,
the ground in frozen wind sweep.

Even coyotes stopped their howl
to huddle down along the creek bed.

We were no warmer before the hearth
where I poked the dim eyes of coal

until they raged at our intrusion.
La, I sang, your face

half glow, half chill against me.
Scorpions scuffled closer to the flame,

their arched, translucent tails
like the scolding fingers of angry men

and outside our locked door, rattlesnakes
curled and uncurled in a moving knot.

La, I sang, and you sang with me,
sweet breath among all these creatures—

until the coyotes slept, the poison
of scorpions boiled dry,

and the snakes, hearing our strong voice,
listened in silence from their sunless rocks.

A Child Wakes in the Night

I lift her, rocking, stroking. Dark room, the heat of our bodies.
Sparkles of light beneath my sleep-swollen lids.

A child's life
is a layered thing, shiny
mica peeled from a rock   a glacier
with its layers of fern,
or a closed hand   with a gift inside.

She carries the dark room's
memory, the warmth of our bodies
a place
for which   there are no words.

Love presses in; we breathe
against wind   we are rising
out of breath from that deep lake.

On Not Loving Your Children

Stop loving them at two.
August nights, when rain comes in the window
and lightning snaps the air,
don't run to them.
Or, if you must, don't look in their eyes,
the clear glass of your own fear.

If you love them at ten,
turn away from baseball, dance class,
or the riding ring. Their slim bodies
split the air like fish.

By sixteen there is no hope.
They circle farther and farther away,
whistling to friends in strange tongues,
shining in skin you don't remember
touching or bathing.

At twenty, they are gone,
the air filled with their mist.
If you love them still, turn on your back,
stare into the sun for their reflections,
swirling and leaping like burning gases,
the sea-swell, the undertow.

Photograph

Daughter by the hollyhock,
in a white dress
with her friends
at eighth grade graduation.

The sun shines on them,
their skin
soft and fragrant as flowers,
and they squint
into my inner eye
that records
this beginning.

My daughter turns
and looks at me
while distances increase,
days and winds stir

the fragile blossoms fall, soft
where she stands.
Her life and my life—
flowers between us, the petals
trembling for the wonderful blooms,

the new gardens, the green summers
I see in her eyes—

the lush summers
that I cannot enter.
We smile.
Go on, I say to her.
Go on.

Suicide Craze

They've done it all over town
with guns at their throats,
ropes in the garage, or pills
and booze. Once in our own backyard
didn't your best friend stumble,
lie down in our pasture
stunned by all her grandmother's pills
and half a bottle of rum?

You cried for her then, rocking her,
holding her head from the soft moisture
of horse dung, shielding her eyes
from the sun, and flies that gathered
like caviar on her lips.

Now each morning,
I look for warnings in your room—
half-eaten pickle, the frail ribs of grapes,
their sweet fruit gone, a glaze of soda
on the bedside stand where it spilled
and you let it dry. I dream
slim bodies wrapped in ambulance sheets,
imagine rope burns
on every tender neck, smell your breath
with every good-night kiss.

Knife, Cucumber, Blood

Daughter, my seed,
my letting go.

Once, hungry, you took a knife
and steadied it to slice the bread.
It slipped, drew a sharp edge
through your own moist flesh—
like paring a cucumber
you said. Then, in pain,
held your hand to your mouth.

Once,
child at my breast,
my own blood
still on my thighs, I was afraid,
with no one to stitch me, to tell me
we taste of dying slowly.
All that night,
the woman in white
read Sunday's newspaper
in a back room.

Live, little one.
Someday you'll know—
we are, mothers, daughters,
the only nurses. We
keep each other
whole, out of danger.

To a Daughter, Moved Away

At home I scrape stars from your ceiling,
stars fixed on a vault of blue
when you were ten, in love
with stars and horses,
the way both seemed bright
and out of reach.

Now I do not hear you
calling out in sleep. You have grown up,
fled to a street of Victorian houses,
weather-ruined, overrun
with kids on skate boards.
We have said goodnight

in the light of Orion;
overhead, invented nebulae,
spun three planets out of orbit
around your horseshow ribbons.

When you looked beyond your window
you thought the sky was dull.

Tonight, Deneb and Rigel
peel from your ceiling easily.
Through different doorways
we see the light of constellations
cooled into darkness a hundred years.

There is nothing
I wouldn't do for you.

Taking the Children Back

August is hot.
Two hens die, one
at the whim of a dog,
the other just seemed entranced,
willing herself to sleep.

I shovel dirt on this small grave
and think back
to my children at birth.

I counted their toes, traced
the tight seam of their skin,
counted the days
that flew from their eyes.

Tell me—
where do children go?

Only a rooster's distant
argument, and the light changing—
everything here as temporary as dust.

I have no choice
but to take them back.

Whole children,
their ribcages slide
into mine, our hearts
tumble together,
our hands intertwine—

together, we cast a single shadow.
Walking the earth, we carry
our memories and our bones.

How I Imagine It

Ahead of me on the road, my daughter
and her husband in their old Subaru.
He's driving and I'm following them to the Danbury garage
to fix the ping that's been there for weeks
when suddenly their car careens, crashes into a tree
and bursts into flames. I park my car, just stop it
and run, run to the door bashed off its frame.
My hands reach in, carefully,
across her silky printed dress, the white-collared one
she likes so much. She is thin
and graceful, I unhook her seat belt,
the silver metal clasp snaps open and the webbing falls away,
her head tilted as if she's sleeping,
but I smell gas, the stink of burning tires.
People cry out, shouting to me, *Get away!* I lean in,
incredibly strong, and lift her up and out,
she is all air, long arms, hands with my knucklebones.
I hold her, wrap her dress around her knees,
her husband lies over the steering wheel, the horn blasting,
like in the movies, and I run, holding her in my arms.
I kneel by the roadside, let her body unfold
in a tree's green shadow, into long stems that smell like cut grass
the summers my father pushed the hand mower and mother
made lemonade, squeezing the lemons in her hands, picking
each seed out. I bend,
knowing if I can save her, I can save myself, if I save her
she will forgive me for everything I have ever done,
for everything I have allowed to be done. I bend
and place my mouth over hers, take in one big breath, breathe it
into her mouth, into lungs that catch, grab it,
hurl it through to her heart, her heart
holds and contracts, once, again, again and she gasps for air.
I feel her warm, every cell ignites and glows, she is

alive.... The light
turns yellow, turns red. Their car slows ahead of me, stops.
The stoplight swings in the wind. It's almost Autumn.

Prayer

O Lord
let my children recall
that I played my guitar, held them
through nightmares
singing *Wynken, Blynken and Nod.*

Let them remember the words
of my heart, the voice of my dreams.
Let them recall that they lived
within walls of my flesh
and that life moves toward death

without thought or regret
on some beautiful night
when a perfectly sung
circle of song
will come round again
as their children are born
and nod through their dreaming,
O Lord.

Everything in Life Is Divided

Everything in life is divided:
twenty-four hours that fade from day to night,

the sand at Martha's Vineyard, where we vacationed last year,
separating us from the ocean

where we swam, then returned to our blanket,
the two of us making one marriage,

sharing the apple sliced to reveal the identical
black seeds of its surprised face.

Even our bodies can be halved, although less evenly:
lungs partitioned into lobes, the heart's blood

pumped from right to left, the brain's two hemispheres
directing our arms, our legs,

our lives into the two possibilities of the Greek mask.
My life's work, too, is divided—

on one side of my desk, unfinished poems;
on the other, nursing books with dog-eared pages.

Aren't we all somehow divided?
Like when my daughter was in labor, my first

grandchild emerging into the room's blue air,
suddenly entering new territory,

and how, when after the delivery my daughter kept bleeding,
I couldn't look at the newborn in the incubator

but stood fast beside my child, the woman who once
slipped from my life into her own and now had divided herself again

while I balanced in my hands *Joy* and *Fear,* cradling them both
until the bleeding stopped.

Croup Weather

A March day surprised by a sudden change
in the Gulf Stream, blue swirls in the sky like currents

on a TV weather map—jacket weather, scarf-off weather.
My daughter tries to shrug it off, but memory is body-linked,

chemicals clicked on when tree limbs scritch
against the kitchen window or a damp chill settles in at dusk.

Her child's sudden one-note cough at 2 a.m. began the rush:
her upturned face, a flash of glassy eyes,

the thermometer's silver finger rising *104, 105*—
the yawning dog, the husband who slept through until

my daughter woke him. Then the air-conditioned ER,
the moonlighting doc who couldn't intubate a throat

that tight, the rescue helicopter grounded by storm,
a special team called from miles away, arriving just in time,

they said, the child blue, almost moribund.
Now, a shift in the wind calls back the respirator's hiss,

those nights in ICU and for weeks after, the child's still-
hoarse, steroid-crazy cries. *But now*, a friend asks,

your girl's all right? My daughter wraps her sweater
tight around her body.

It Was the Second Patient of the Day

It was the second patient of the day
whose arm reminded me of my daughter's arm,

and so I wanted to touch the firm flesh
along the ulnar ridge and the soft skin in the elbow's bend

and press my lips to the few freckles,
to the sweet and salt taste of my daughter.

Then it was the nape of a young man's neck,
how, when he turned away, a twin ridge of muscle

rose to create a hollow where the close-cut hairs lie,
and so I wanted to kiss the nape of my son's neck

and inhale the scent of him,
a trace of autumn air and rivers.

Later it was the hands of the girl with the injured wrist,
how shiny her fingernails, how the tendons moved

over her metacarpals like violin strings,
reminding me of my granddaughters' hands,

and so I wanted to twine my fingers
with theirs, to savor the tiny pulse in the thumb's web.

The last patient of the day had my grandson's gaze,
patient as a quiet sea—

and so I wanted to hold my grandson's face to mine,
to see, reflected in his green eyes, all these images

repeating themselves into infinity.

Little Children then, on My Lap

Their bodies rested
against my breast
like innocent lovers
carelessly brushing skin to skin,
a slip of space in time—
gestures caught,
fossil impressions:
our eyes, our hair
different shades
of the same dark grain.

Within my ribs
the echo of their hearts,
our chance meeting.

Now, when I stand,
my hands cup
the empty space
all mothers carry.

I have searched everywhere
for proof—
my flesh still hot
where their heads pressed,
pale marks
from a small hip,
spittle,
strands of their hair
urgently clinging—
anything.

II.

It won't last,
of course. The sun

at just this angle
on the coral tulips.

—Ellen Bass

Windmill

My daughter gave me a little statue,
a windmill, copper and bronze,

because there are windmills in Kansas
where she lives now, the wind there always

blowing hot across fields of soy or wheat,
in winter howling over dirt roads.

I keep the windmill on my desk because
she said it would remind me of her,

and it does, it turns in my mind bringing
her to me, her cancer I cannot cure,

the suffering that rages a storm
through her body. I pace round and round

but the arms of the little windmill
do not move. Instead, I wait for the winds

from Kansas—the warm breeze of her voice,
the anticipation of her days—

to waft and tumble to me across
the span of earth and time between us.

III.

All things hang like a drop of dew
upon a blade of grass.

—W. B. Yeats

The First Weeks

January 2020

There's a new virus, just a cold, someone says,
so my son works, carries on like normal,
and my daughter who lives far away finds
another tumor in the same breast as last time,
that means the lumpectomy and chemo did nothing,
she says, and her doctor orders another mammogram.

I visit four pharmacies searching for hand
sanitizer, buy plenty of zinc lozenges, and
my daughter's mammogram shows a new mass
with its ragged cancer edges. *So the radiation
didn't do anything either*, she says. The first
viral cases are verified in the U.S. No one has

died yet and the new tumor is not yet removed.
She says, *I know they'll want me to do more chemo,
but I'm saying no*, and I order a dozen masks
from Etsy, two 1000-piece puzzles, print out
"Rules for staying safe during a pandemic"
and hang them on my refrigerator door.

The Second Month

February 2020

My daughter is in Topeka, lying on the narrow bed
that will carry her into the dark mouth of the MRI, IV contrast

flooding her veins. I hope they have covered her ears,
tamping the clang of the magnets that magically pull apart

and reassemble her body's tissues and flesh, looking for cancer's
spread. I can't fly to her, can't risk catching or bringing the virus,

asking her to tend me, when I should be tending her. While I wait
for her tests results, I'll walk outside, wave to neighbors who also

may be too far away from grown children who still need tending,
still need to be called in from a day of pain and bathed clean,

who may not ask but still want that old story read to them,
the one in which everyone is safe and there will be a tomorrow—

after the closet is swept free of monsters, after the curtains
are closed in the nightlight's glow, after all the good-nights are said,

and *I love you* is the last thing they hear as we close the door.

Amazing

Late March 2020

It's amazing, the President says,
the job we're doing. Everyone will be

back to work by Easter, and on the news
82,000 are infected, more than in China

or Italy, our doctors and nurses
without enough masks, eye shields,

not enough ventilators and too many
deaths, and my daughter's MRI verified

two new cancers in the same breast
where the first tumor was removed.

Amazing that back in 1894 two men,
Halsted and Meyer, pioneered a radically

invasive surgery, shucked an entire
cancerous breast from a woman's chest,

stripped the pectoralis major, gutted
the axilla, the nodes, and women survived,

scarred but cancer free. Two days ago
a doctor sliced away my daughter's breast,

the one that nursed four children, the one
betrayed by statistics that say women

who nurse rarely get breast cancer,
and while some of the 82,000 infected

might die alone tonight, my daughter
goes home, chest bound tight in white gauze,

a rubber drain pulling bloody fluid
from her sudden, amazing emptiness.

Borders

April 2020

The borders to Mexico and Canada
are closed, but here in Connecticut

the ICU beds are filled with New Yorkers
who daily spill over the line, fleeing Brewster

and Yonkers to second homes, to more
available hospital beds and by April tenth

1,677,256 are infected and 101,732 dead—
don't we know this virus knows no boundaries,

just as cancer can't be sequestered, no imaginary
barrier keeps malignant cells from their journey

from breast to bone, to brain or lung, to any tissue
made vulnerable by genes or fate or even by God?

A God who in his power must have permitted
this plague, allowed our descent into solitude

and fear, the same God to whom I now bow down,
to whom I raise my voice in prayer: *kind* God,

in your mercy whisper in the midst of chaos
that my daughter's breast, cut away, will have,

under the pathologist's microscope, clean borders,
no errant cells, not one invisible threat stepped

over the line, not one let loose into another
country, not today, please God, and not tomorrow.

What a Terrible Mistake

Early May 2020

What a terrible mistake, that big funeral in NYC,
the dinner party in Westport, the man who
didn't feel well but got on the plane anyway, rays

of illness like searing spokes of the sun, like the
sharp spikes of a medieval torture wheel,
and the count today 3.88 million infected, 271,000

dead, who knows how many unaccounted for.
Mistakes get made, and how about this for a mistake,
when a surgeon removes a breast but misses

the tumors within, just one little statistic in a litany
of misery unless you are the one with
the same two small cancers showing up again

on yet another MRI, ultrasound, PET scan, physical
exam, and so right now my daughter is in surgery
once more, *what a terrible mistake*, her oncologist said,

and the pathologist agreed, *yes, same cancer,
left behind*, and now there's a new little spot
right lung, upper lobe, they'll follow it

in four weeks with x-rays, more scans, but first
    let's get this woman back into surgery
fix if we can this terrible, terrible mistake.

Opening

June 2020

—now the cautious world begins to relax,
just a bit, social gatherings of five,
masked and distanced, senior hours at the market

abolished, then in June, hair salons and barber shops,
gatherings of ten, etc., etc., the slow
opening of society while a new surgeon opens

my daughter's chest for the second time since
the failed mastectomy. First, a surgery to capture
tumors the incompetent doctor missed, next

a second operation because *cancer cells were seen
at the margins*, so this time the surgeon cuts
through muscle down to bone, and today, while we

wait to hear if any cancer cells still linger invading
the borders, her chest wall stripped so tight
my child can barely lift her arm, she calls me, excited,

a new project, a barn quilt, a 4x4 foot pattern
she will paint—*I want colors*, she says,
dark and light blue, greens, even some cranberry—

and display on the old barn at the beginning
of their long driveway, one I've walked so many times,
a journey that starts here in my heart, meanders

1400 miles to her open door, so many possibilities
to choose from: *flying geese, hourglass, diamond in
the center—Kansas troubles, mother's dream, broken dish.*

Statistics

Late July 2020

Statistically fewer than one percent of
breast cancers are metaplastic triple-
negative, a type that can't be treated
with hormones, only with chemo,

although no chemo really works and
survival odds are dismal, this particular
cancer (like the virus) is an expert at stealth,
spreading before you even know it's there,

and on my daughter's latest scans,
tumors have invaded both lungs,
her scapula, parts of the spine, all lighting
up on film like bright, burning nebulae.

Stage four now, the doctor tells her,
some women might last a year or so
and soon I'll fly to Kansas, to my daughter,
keeper of these terrible statistics

in the midst of this damn pandemic,
during which the danger of flying
and lingering in airports is *moderately high*
(in the USA 4,339,997 now infected

and 148,866 dead, no stats for those
living with chronic disease, the aftermath),
so when I arrive I must wear a mask,
must not touch my daughter, cannot hold

or kiss her, can't play the odds of *what
if I hug her but* don't *give her the virus*
so while I wait out the days until
I leave to fly to my daughter's side,

I watch baby elephants throwing tantrums
on You Tube and play *solitaire* which was once
called *patience*, a game that can be won with
no risk of embracing or infecting anyone.

Taking Risks

August 2020

1.

My husband and I risk three airports, two flights (people
with masks below their noses, under their chins, scrunched

on their laps) so we can get to my daughter's Kansas town
where nobody seems to believe there's a virus

even with more than six million infected and 183,141 deaths.
I get it, everyone is tired of this pandemic,

and my daughter's tired of having cancer, tired of consults
with Sloane Kettering, M.D. Anderson, KU Med,

in person or via zoom, tired of the oncologists' endless drone
there's no chemo or immunotherapy that will help, tired of friends

pushing her to take risks, sending her articles on alternative
"sure cures." My daughter rules out 714X, knows it's a hoax,

won't risk chewing apricot pits or taking B17, doesn't think standing
barefoot on the earth really beams healing impulses to shatter cancers.

2.

When we arrive at her front door, while I hang back,
she rushes forward unafraid, embraces me, and the four
grandchildren join her, throw their arms around us.
And all week in Kansas we pretend there is no cancer, only

the chocolate chip cookies we bake and eat, the late summer
flowers in the botanical gardens at the university,
the silly movies we watch on Netflix, all of us
on the couch with the dog Finn and Baby Kitty

and Gray Kitty. We drive to a bigger town,
find a cute boutique where I buy my daughter
hand soap and she buys a table runner for next summer,
birds and vines for a meal in a world in which

we imagine there might be no tumors, a future that
holds only joy. Then, before the last day of our visit,
she drives us miles over dirt roads to a hill crest
overlooking the Kaw Valley. *It reminds me of Ireland,*

she says, pulls up to The Old Stone Church,
dedicated in 1882, shows us the plot she has selected
and paid for, how it faces the slow grassy dip into the valley—
how it is and forever will be there under the big Kansas sky.

3.

Returning from my daughter's town and the graveyard
that guards the Kaw Valley, my husband and I wait again

in three airports, sit masked and silent through two flights,
and home in Connecticut quarantine for two weeks

during which I don't dare risk post office or grocery store,
instead spend hours looking at photos—

my daughter, her kids, arms linked and smiling—
and search the Internet for last ditch ideas. Would she

consider fenbendazole, a drug around for forty years?
Or bee sting therapy? The days drag. The months are flying by.

Counting

Late September 2020

More than 200,000 in the U.S. have died
of COVID or its complications
and seven days a week my daughter
wakes with her cancer, finds new masses,
firm visible lumps under her skin
at the site of her mastectomy. Her oncologist
wants to try off-label chemo or maybe a new
double-blind drug trial in which the white cells
of eighty percent of women crash and burn,
requiring certain hospitalization but no guarantee
how many more weeks would be gained.
No, she tells him. *I'm alive, and I want to
enjoy whatever time is left. God has a plan
so deep it's hard to understand.*

In October there will be two full moons,
a harvest moon that shines only every three
years and a blue moon on All Hallows' Eve.
In December, month of the cold moon,
my daughter will be fifty-four.
We will see thirteen full moons in 2021,
and today in the ninth month I offer this poem
that has twenty-nine lines, two hundred
and ten words, each syllable a prayer
that my daughter will live to dream under
wolf moon, snow moon, worm moon,
pink moon, strawberry moon, buck moon,
sturgeon moon, corn moon, hunters' moon,
beaver moon, under flower moon
for countless days, for years without number.

Bargaining

The last day of October 2020

It snowed yesterday, a sparkly squall.

Tonight we turn back the clocks, falling behind again.
Last month the doctor said my daughter might live

another year. *You look really good*, he told her,
considering. And so we bargain:

J. lived two years with stage four cancer, my daughter says,
and P. more than two years after her thyroid cancer spread.

And my dad, he lasted two years with stage four bladder cancer.
More people are living with cancer now,

my daughter tells me, *than are dying of it.*
As of this morning, in the U.S., two hundred

and twenty-nine thousand, six hundred eighty-six have died
of COVID, probably more than that by now.

And if only everyone wears a mask, if everyone
pays attention to social distancing, if bars close

and food is take-out and Plexiglas works
and we all get tested then maybe…

I hate this fucking virus, my daughter tells me.
She pulls her youngest out of school, a COVID hot spot.

I'll home school her, like I did the others—two years
until she graduates. Two years. I don't have five, but maybe two?

Radical Gratitude

Thanksgiving Day 2020

In the U.S., now more than 256,000 have died
of COVID-19. So far, my children,

my grandchildren, my husband, me—we are safe.
And all month I've been trying to practice

radical gratitude for this safety,
for the vaccines that may soon be ready,

for a newly elected not-yet-in office president,
for the nurses who pierced my daughter's

veins, for the toxic red chemo that did
not help her, not even a little, for how

today's glossy, crimson cranberries
brought all this back and made me weep.

Most of all, I'm thankful for my daughter's
beautiful smile when we FaceTimed last week,

for her strong voice when she told me
about the new hip pain, the elevated enzymes

that signal more bone damage, the mild
narcotic prescribed *just in case,*

for the phone number for Palliative Care,
although the doctor said, *you're not ready*

for hospice just yet. I'm thankful too that
once I studied poetry with Yehuda Amichai,

an Israeli poet, now long dead. In Jerusalem,
young soldiers going to war carried his poems

in their pockets. And I'm grateful
for the poems I'm writing, as if by writing

them I might stop my daughter's cancer,
trap its destruction in words,

like scorpions embedded in amber.
In class, I wrote down everything

Yehuda taught. *When words fail,* he said,
that's when poetry begins. And yet, he added,

*in the midst of violent conflict, in times
of greatest suffering, even poems can't save us.*

Winter Solstice

December 21, 2020

Tonight the air had the scent of earth, of dust,
like old books in a sunlit library rarely used.

We drove out to an overlook facing southwest,
hoping to see Jupiter and Saturn in conjunction,

the Star of Bethlehem—but it was too cloudy.
We waited twenty minutes, then went home.

Earlier, I'd worked for hours on my daughter's obituary.
She'd sent me notes on her hobbies, where she'd been

employed, how her greatest joy was raising
her four children. The funeral home thought it best,

she said, to get these details in place, not to wait
until the last minute. I don't know her cancer's plan,

don't know when the last minute will come,
but considering the year ahead, I see no stars guiding

the way, only the opened earth, the drag and drudge
of grief. Where are the other mothers who have lost

their daughters, who might be my guides and mentors?
Where are my helpers, now that I need them?

The Sacrament of Time

The last day of December 2020

December, month of my daughter's birth,
and this morning, day of my daughter's
latest CT scan, urgently done before

the New Year, results reported urgently:
lung cancers are growing, *rapid increase,*
and in the liver, *innumerable tumors.*

This year, 19,923,169 were diagnosed
with COVID; more than 400,000 have died,
and I'm ashamed not to feel more sorrow

but right now, all I can mourn is the coming
death of one. Born in Texas, in a small town
hospital with twenty rooms, brick walls, cactus

growing in gardens of white, crushed stone,
she was my first. The nurse left me alone
in the labor room and when the pains

became too great I called *nurse nurse*
but she was in the back, coffee cup, newspaper,
run down scuffed white shoes, white uniform

tight around her ample, slow body. I climbed
over the bed rails, stood crying, *something
is happening.* Baby's head right there, delivery

imminent, rush me back to bed, my doctor
was unavailable, she said, so in the hallway—
early morning hallway, some patients arriving,

nurses, a few doctors—she stopped one,
urged him in to catch my daughter just as she
was born, pink and bawling, dried off, bound

and whisked away. Later, unwrapped
in my room, all perfection; in the nursery,
the only baby. I stood at the glass window,

watching. The next day her father and I
took her home to an A-frame house on a hill—
no heat, no phone—an adventure overlooking

Canyon Lake. In our yard, a single century plant
bloomed. When our daughter was six weeks old,
we drove back to Connecticut. I held her

in my arms—front seat, no seatbelts to protect us,
miles of highway and the hum of tires, her
small voice of hunger, of sleep. *Poems cannot*

save us, Amichai said, but all I have are these poems,
flimsy containers to hold the joy of her life,
to build a border around a grief too great to bear.

And yet, in the writing, time has become
a sacrament: memories of each day,
every hour, and now the living presence of each

new day, every new hour given us, until there is
one last journey left to take with my daughter.
I will hold her in my arms all the way home.

About the Author

Cortney Davis is the author of four full-length poetry collections, three poetry chapbooks, three memoirs and co-editor of three anthologies of creative writing by nurses. Honors include an NEA Poetry Grant, three CT Commission on the Arts Poetry Grants, two CT Center for the Book Awards, the Prairie Schooner Book Award, an Independent Publisher's Benjamin Franklin Gold Medal in Non-Fiction, and six Books of the Year first place awards in the category of creative works from the *American Journal of Nursing*. www.cortneydavis.com

She says, "For as long as I can remember, I've written poems—poems about my childhood, my parents, my children and grandchildren, about my many years working as a nurse. Poetry has been, for me, a way to honor our amazing human experiences; to accept contradiction and to invite the transcendent; a way to walk alongside grief while still reaching out for every moment of joy. When sorrow seemed too great to bear, the poems in this collection served to contain both anguish and hope; to record and comfort; to cherish and remember; and to affirm that love and life are everlasting."

CPSIA information can be obtained
at www.ICGtesting.com
Printed in the USA
LVHW110445300821
696425LV00008B/587

9 781736 416839